# THE JEFF HEALEY BAND

MW00813192

# HELL TO PAY

## CONTENTS

Full Color Fold-Out
Follows Page 64

As recorded by THE JEFF HEALEY BAND on ARISTA Records

Management: Forte Records and Productions Ltd.
Edited by Jeff Jacobson
Music Engraving by W.R. Music
Production Manager: Daniel Rosenbaum
Art Direction: Alisa Hill
Administration Monica Corton
Director of Music: Mark Phillips

*Photography by Dimo Safari*

ISBN: 0-89524-600-7

Copyright © 1990 Cherry Lane Music Company, Inc.
International Copyright Secured   All Rights Reserved

CHERRY LANE MUSIC:   THE PRINT COMPANY

**EXECUTIVE:** Michael Lefferts, President; Kathleen A. Maloney, Director of Advertising and Promotion; Len Handler, Creative Services Manager; Monica Corton, Contracts Administrator; Karen Carey, Division Secretary
**MUSIC:** Mark Phillips, Director of Music; Jon Chappell, Associate Director of Music; Jeff Jacobson, Music Editor; Steve Gorenberg, Music Editor.
**ART:** Alisa Hill, Art Director; Kerstin Fairbend, Assistant Art Director.
**PRODUCTION:** Daniel Rosenbaum, Production Manager; Betty Chasan, Production Assistant.

# THE JEFF HEALEY BAND

## INTRODUCTION

Can a Blue Boy Sing the Whites? With the phenomenal ascent in the past three years and two albums of the young, blind, white Canadian blues guitar player Jeff Healey, the question has been put before the house of music once again, and once again the answer is an unequivocal "Yeah, sure. Why not?"

The Whites, more descriptively known as The Suburban Mid-Century White Young American Blues, have been a viable and enduring form of music probably since the mid 50's, although its first real surge of popularity did not occur until the early 60's. Before then, whatever blue boys there were of the white persuasion defined their urges via the more acceptable vessel of country music. But where Hank Williams and Merle Travis adapted the Whites into an ongoing tradition, Elvis Presley and Jerry Lee Lewis carved it into a tradition of their own, ultimately leading to rock 'n' roll as a perfectly respectable receptacle for their unrespectable feelings.

In the 60's, however, with rock 'n' roll having been shaved of much of its early primal power, like an etherized patient about to be castrated, the Whites began to infest a variety of suburban neighbor-hoods across the nation, like a new form of Boogie Woogie Flu. In New York City, John Hammond Jr. strapped his axe across his hog and took off for the bottom with his running shoes. In Chicago, Michael Bloomfield was spending his (copious) allowance on all the blues records he could find, in preparation for his fateful meeting with fellow native Paul Butterfield. Down in Daytona Beach, Florida, Gregg and Duane, the brothers Allman, were growing up, growing their own. Outside of Washington, D.C., Roy Buchanan had had the Whites for quite some time. In San Francisco, Bob Weir, Jerry Garcia and Jorma Kaukonen contracted the Whites around the same time they began mixing LSD with their Gary Davis licks. In and around London, England, Mick Jagger offered a pretty pale imitation of the Whites; but guys like Robert Plant, Jimmy Page and Jeff Beck were more authentic. And then there was Eric Clapton, perhaps the first blue *man* to sing the Whites. Later we had Al Kooper's early Blood, Sweat and Tears, Danny Kalb and the Blues Project, the nasal David Bromberg, and Johnny Winter, arguably the whitest White singer on record. Could a blue girl sing the Whites? Listen to Janis Joplin, Tracy Nelson, Bonnie Raitt.

Obviously basing their laments on musical structures already laid down on record by some of the same black forebears who gave them the seeds for rock 'n' roll—your basic King family (B.B., Freddy and Albert ... but not Don), Muddy Waters, Albert Collins, Bo Diddley—these early singers of the Whites, while deprived the natural outlet of historical servitude, institutionalized prejudice, and congenital poverty, nevertheless possessed an unalienable need to express their own uniquely hopeless human condition, primarily their singular inability to heed their mothers' basic warning to not get involved in a relationship with someone who had more problems than they had. Plagued by society's doubts about their rights to even sing the Whites, these young, middle class scions of the baby boom dropped out of college, grew their hair to unseemly lengths, and proceeded to make their stringed and vocal instruments screech and howl unlike any before them in the annals of blues, jazz, rhythm 'n' blues, folk or country music. The endless guitar solo was upon us: the primordial wail floating o'er its head eschewed the simple "My baby done left me" for the much more White-sounding "My baby done left me emotionally bankrupt and unable to truly give or receive affection ... I think."

With the intervening decades, the Whites did not vanish, as many had presumed, into the caterwauling caverns of heavy metal, rock 'n' roll's latter-day Led Zeppelin legacy. Avenues of expression like thrash and rap have opened up, hacked from boredom's computer-age dead air of shopping mall towns and synthesized culture, that could have successfully neutered the need to feel the unexpressible beauty and pain of the Whites. But children of the 70's like New Jersey's Southside Johnny and England's Elvis Costello had their pioneering role models to see them through; MTV's limited coverage of the Whites made the 80's imagination palpable, if irrelevant. But it gave us Stevie Ray Vaughan (from Austin) and Huey Lewis (from San Francisco) and John Hiatt (from Nashville by way of Indianapolis) to carry on the tradition. Mick Hucknall, that blue boy from London in Simply Red, sure can sing the Whites.

And now, entering the 10th decade of the 20th century, we find that Canada has been cultivating its own strain of the Whites. Previously known for its paucity of White warblers and encompassing a strange gamut from Neil Young to Robbie Robertson to Gordon Lightfoot to Tony Springer, the Canadian tradition is so meager in this area that its most major contribution to the realms of the Whites learned how to play the guitar on his lap, like a piano. Born blind, young Jeff Healey can't be faulted for this lapse. In fact, like all true heroes, he turned a double disadvantage into a monstrous franchise, forging his early Clapton influences into a pair of awesome works of the pentatonic scale: *See the Light* and the current *Hell to Pay*. Feel free to copy his solos at will.

"Learning solos is so beneficial to the beginning guitar player," says Jeff. "I know a lot of guys who don't want to copy anybody's solo. They suffer because they start off with no background. They try to let their fingers and an undeveloped musical mind do the work for them, and they can't. You need the background. I've always told people who ask me about learning improvisation to learn somebody's solo backwards and forwards. Play them a few times and then start doing it in different keys and mixing up the ideas in the solo. The next thing you know, you're improvising."

The emotional terrain on *Hell to Pay* will be familiar to students of the Whites because it focuses on the famous Seven Stages of Unrequited Love: loving too much ("I Think I Love You Too Much"), loving too little ("How Long Can a Man Be Strong," which Steve Cropper might have written for Al Kooper), unattainable love ("I Can't Get My Hands on You"), unbearable love ("Something to Hold on To"), overbearing love ("How Much"), schizoid love ("Full Circle"), and cosmic surrender ("Let It All Go," which John Hiatt might have written for Huey Lewis), before Healey expands his horizons from the purely personal to the universal, with "Highway of Dreams," "Life Beyond the Sky," the Claptonesque "Hell to Pay," and a wonderful cover of The Beatles' "While My Guitar Gently Weeps."

If Healey's case of the Whites is by now thoroughly time honored and traditional, his guitar style is totally his own. "Some people have ignorantly said, `That's a neat gimmick you got there, teaching yourself to play guitar on your lap,'" ruminates Healey. "I say, `I didn't try it as a gimmick. I can't play like everybody else.' I never thought about what I was doing, I just sort of did it. Only now, when people start to ask about it, and I don't have an answer, am I starting to think more about what I'm doing."

Sounds like he's going to have the Whites for a good long time to come.

-Bruce Pollock
Co-Editor-in-Chief
GUITAR *For The Practicing Musician*

# FULL CIRCLE

Words and Music by
Jeff Healey, Joe Rockman
and Tom Stephen

Copyright © 1989 See The Light Music, Inc.
This Arrangement © 1990 See The Light Music, Inc.
International Copyright Secured   All Rights Reserved

3rd Verse
w/Rhy. Fig. 2

It's hard to get you_ out of my   head.        I   try to set   my - self     free._

But just like_ a bad_ hab - it,            you al - ways catch  up  with  me.   Yeah!_

Fill 7

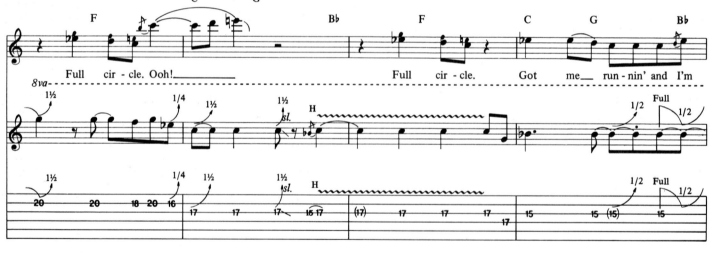

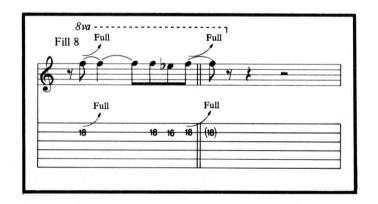

*wah on as filter

*Additional Lyrics*

2. When you cruise down the boulevard,
   All the guys know your name.
   You get their engines runnin', yeah.
   They're all sparked by your flame.

*2nd Pre-chorus:* You tempt me with your burnin' fire,
   Lost in my desire. Yeah.
   You don't know what you've put me through.
   It keeps me spinnin' when I can't have you. *(To Chorus)*

# I THINK I LOVE YOU TOO MUCH

Words and Music by
Mark Knopfler

Copyright © 1990 Straightjacket Songs Limited (PRS)
All Rights Administered by Rondor Music (London) Ltd. (PRS)/
Almo Music Corp. (ASCAP) Administered in the U.S. and Canada
International Copyright Secured  Made in U.S.A.
All Rights Reserved

much.____ If I picked you up, you know you'd

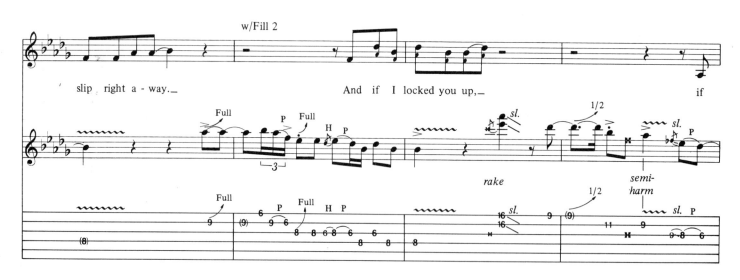

slip right a - way.____ And if I locked you up,____ if

**Bridge**

Guess I'm gon-na get you what you want,___ 'cause I'm so in-to you.___

You don't ev-en give an inch to me, ba-by, though I've been giv-en you a mile or two. Yeah!

Guitar solo
w/Rhy. Fig. 1 (4 times)

*hold bend*    *grad. release*    *trem. bar*

*Depress bar before
striking note.

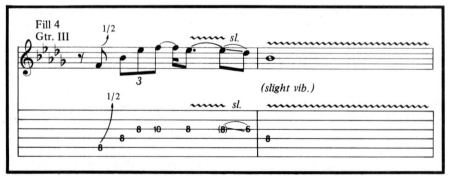

Fill 4
Gtr. III

*(slight vib.)*

Yeah, yeah,___ yeah,___ I'm not a -

You're sit - tin' right there.    How come___ I get the feel - in'___

lone,___ no.

*Slide up neck past
end of fretboard.

Gtr. III

3rd Verse

w/Rhy. Fig. 2
w/Rhy. Fig. 1
w/Rhy. Fig. 3
w/Rhy. Fig. 1
w/Rhy. Fig. 1 (4 times)

18

that you can van-ish in-to the air.___ An' I love___ you more than an-y-bod-y

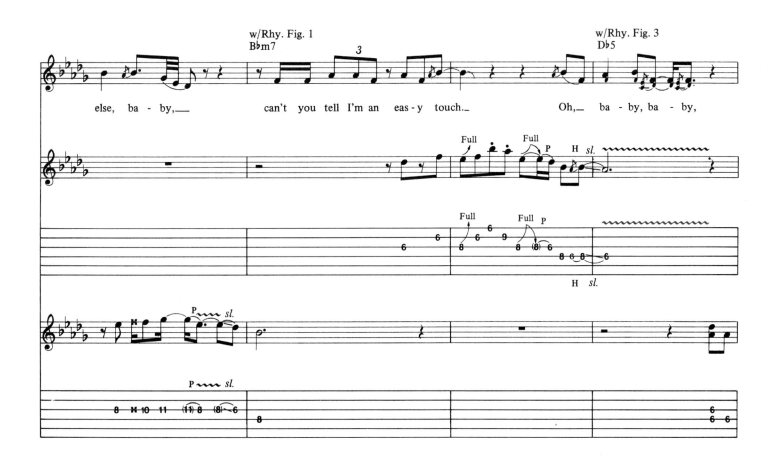

else, ba-by,___ can't you tell I'm an eas-y touch.___ Oh,___ ba-by, ba-by,

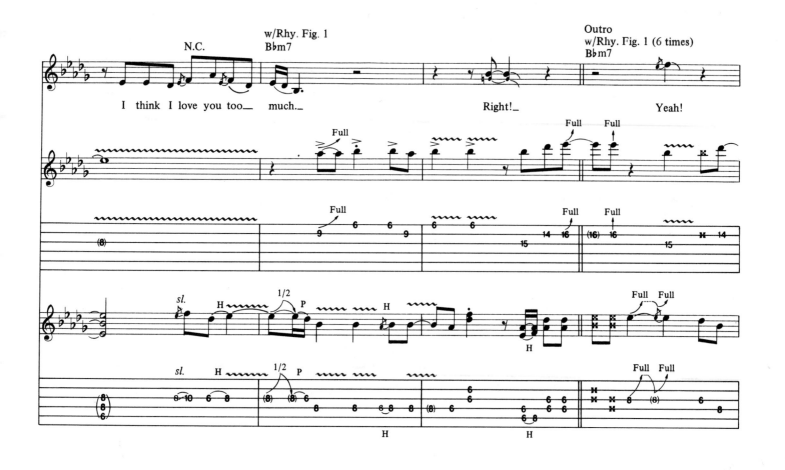

I think I love you too___ much.___          Right!_          Yeah!

Yeah!_          Ha!

(Spoken) Ah,___ truck on __ down.    Heh, heh.                                                Yeah!_

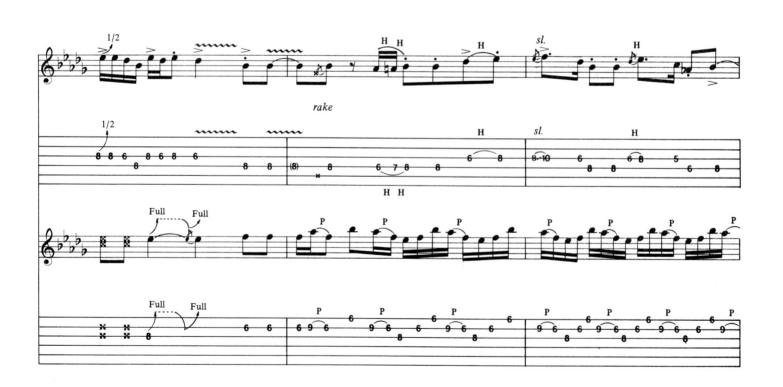

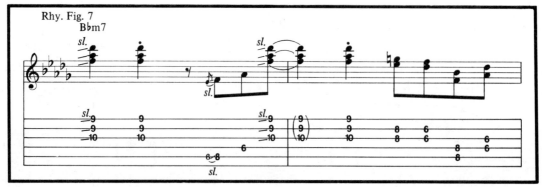

# I CAN'T GET MY HANDS ON YOU

Words and Music by
Jeff Healey

Copyright © 1989 See The Light Music, Inc.
This Arrangement © 1990 See The Light Music, Inc.
International Copyright Secured  All Rights Reserved

*Higher gtr. indicated to left of slashes in TAB.

*Additional Lyrics*

2. Once I loaned out a whole lot of money
   To a man who I called my friend.
   And he skipped town without payin' me back.
   Well, he'll never pull that trick again.
   You know it ain't always been this easy.
   I've worked hard to get to this spot.
   And all that it took was determination
   To get all the things that I've got. *(To Chorus)*

# HOW LONG CAN A MAN BE STRONG

Words and Music by
Steve Cropper and Jimmy Scott

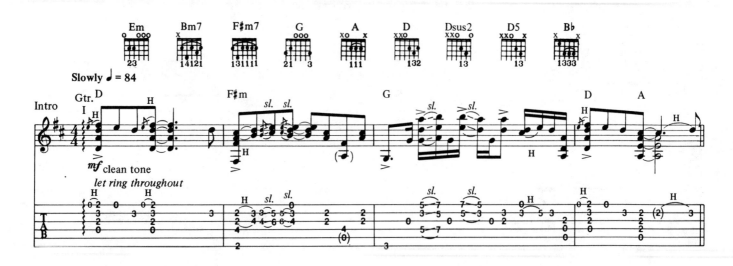

Copyright © 1989, 1990 Midnight Hour Music/Chrysalis Songs (BMI)/Ackee Music, Inc., Left Handed Songs
(3500 West Olive Avenue, Suite 200, Burbank, CA 91503)
International Copyright Secured  All Rights Reserved

lone in this world.__ Still I know she's out_there_ some-where, so I'm gon-na keep_on try - in'.__

Some day I'm gon-na find her, it's just a mat - ter of time. __

*Gtr. IV indicated to left of slashes in TAB.

*Gtr. I indicated to left of slash in TAB.

*Gtr. I indicated to right of slash in TAB.

# LET IT ALL GO

Words and Music by
John Hiatt

Copyright © 1990 Whistling Moon Traveler Music and Careers Music, Inc. (BMI)
International Copyright Secured  All Rights Reserved

## Additional Lyrics

2. I knew a girl who left home in a hurry,
Something to prove and bridges to burn.
Her parents' dreams soon turned into worry.
Angels taught that girl what she needed to learn. *(To Chorus)*

3. I swear to God that it don't come easy,
Can't get it myself most of the time.
I need help to keep the wheels greasy.
Keep that train whistlin' all down the line. *(To Chorus)*

# HELL TO PAY

Words and Music by
Jeff Healey, Joe Rockman
and Tom Stephen

Copyright © 1989 See The Light Music, Inc.
This Arrangement © 1990 See The Light Music, Inc.
International Copyright Secured  All Rights Reserved

peo - ple in the world to - day___ who don't have - a noth - in' but

hell ___ to pay. ___ Yeah. ___

3. Now when your

'Cause you know,    prob - lems come and prob - lems go.___

This is some - thing you should know.    There's peo - ple in the world to - day___

who don't    have - a noth - in' but    hell___ to pay.___ 4. Now, if you

## Additional Lyrics

3. Now, when your life of success has you living in doubt
And you're feeling like there's nowhere to turn,
Just remember the world that you don't know about
And all the lessons that you can learn. *(To Chorus)*

4. Now, when you think you've got problems you don't really need,
They're really not as bad as they seem.
In a world full of misery from hatred and greed,
Your problems are another man's dream. *(To Chorus)*

# WHILE MY GUITAR GENTLY WEEPS

Words and Music by
George Harrison

*Two gtrs. arr. for one.

*T = Thumb

*Gtr. I is doubled by acous. gtr. throughout.

Copyright © 1968 Harrisongs Ltd.
This Arrangement © 1990 Harrisongs Ltd.
International Copyright Secured  All Rights Reserved

Cherry Lane Music

Courtesy of Arista Records

Courtesy of Arista Records

# SOMETHING TO HOLD ON TO

Words and Music by
Jeff Healey

Copyright © 1989 See The Light Music, Inc.
This Arrangement © 1990 See The Light Music, Inc.
International Copyright Secured  All Rights Reserved

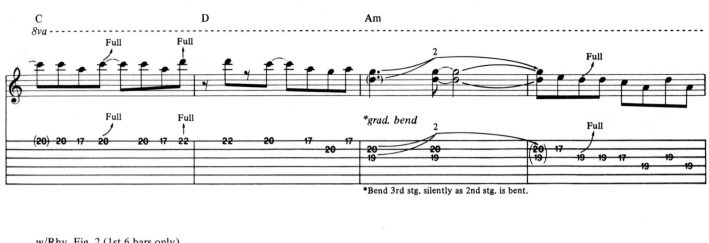

*Bend 3rd stg. silently as 2nd stg. is bent.

w/Rhy. Fig. 2 (1st 6 bars only)

w/Rhy. Fig. 1 (2 times)

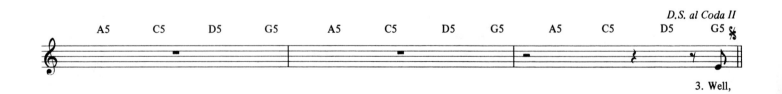

*D.S. al Coda II*

3. Well,

## Additional Lyrics

2. She never thought she'd be this lonely.
   She thought that she was the one and only for him.
   He would never run away.
   But then he left without a warning.
   And ever since that sad, dreary morning,
   Her heart has been mending day by day. *(To Chorus)*

3. Now she's got her strength together.
   She can feel a change in the weather for her.
   She knows where her head's at.
   So forget all those romantic notions
   And get control of all your emotions
   'Cause she ain't ready for nothing like that. *(To Chorus)*

# HOW MUCH

Words and Music by
John Daniel Tate and Gregg Sutton

Copyright © 1989, 1990 Ackee Music, Inc., John Daniel Tate Music
(3500 West Olive Avenue, Suite 200, Burbank, CA 91505)/Irving Music, Inc./Doolittle Music (BMI)
International Copyright Secured  All Rights Reserved

How much love— do you want from— me? How— much love— do you

want from— me?— Ooh.—

# HIGHWAY OF DREAMS

Words and Music by
Jeff Healey, Joe Rockman
and Tom Stephen

1. Fac-es_ and plac-es_ in mo-tion_ be-come all_ the_ same._____
2.3. *See additional lyrics*

Wide o-pen spac-es_ and cit-ies_ with-out an-y____ name._____

Peo-ple_ who gam-ble in search of_ their quest, jok-ers_ and ac-es_ all put to_ the test.__

Copyright © 1989 See The Light Music, Inc.
This Arrangement © 1990 See The Music, Inc.
International Copyright Secured  All Rights Reserved

*vol. swells

*vol. swell

*Additional Lyrics*

2. Ladies all painted in shades of a haunting despair.
   Men who are tainted by life that appears so unfair.
   Here comes a man in his new Cadillac,
   Women and wine and a pool in the back.
   Winners and losers all travel the highway of dreams. *(To Bridge)*

3. Factories once proud of their work long ago have closed down.
   Parks that were loud now have silenced the merry-go-round.
   People who dwell in their castles of steel,
   Visions of progress have now become real.
   Winners and losers all travel the highway of dreams, *etc.*

# LIFE BEYOND THE SKY

Words and Music by
Jeff Healey, Joe Rockman
and Tom Stephen

Copyright © 1989 See The Light Music, Inc.
This Arrangement © 1990 See The Music, Inc.
International Copyright Secured  All Rights Reserved

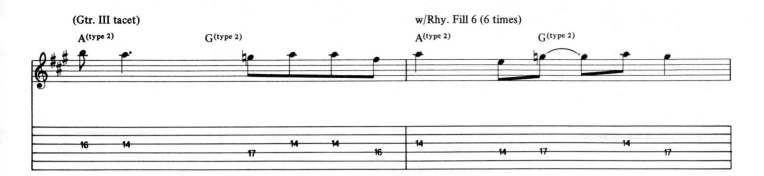

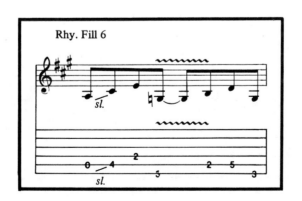

*Gtr. II: Substitute Asus2 & fade out by end of next bar.

Fdbk. pitch:E

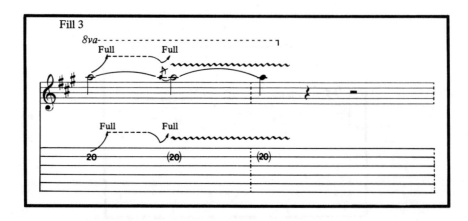

Fill 3

# TABLATURE EXPLANATION

**TABLATURE:** A six-line staff that graphically represents the guitar fingerboard, with the top line indicating the highest sounding string (high E). By placing a number on the appropriate line, the string and fret of any note can be indicated. The number 0 represents an open string. For example:

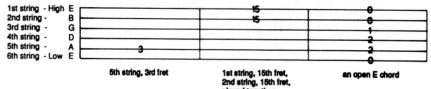

| | |
|---|---|
| 1st string - High E | |
| 2nd string - B | |
| 3rd string - G | |
| 4th string - D | |
| 5th string - A | |
| 6th string - Low E | |

5th string, 3rd fret

1st string, 15th fret, 2nd string, 15th fret, played together

an open E chord

## Definitions for Special Guitar Notation

**BEND:** Strike the note and bend up ½ step (one fret).

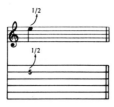

**BEND:** Strike the note and bend up a whole step (two frets).

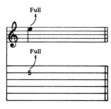

**BEND AND RELEASE:** Strike the note and bend up ½ (or whole) step, then release the bend back to the original note. All three notes are tied, only the first note is struck.

**PRE-BEND:** Bend the note up ½ (or whole) step, then strike it.

**PRE-BEND AND RELEASE:** Bend the note up ½ (or whole) step. Strike it and release the bend back to the original note.

**UNISON BEND:** Strike the two notes simultaneously and bend the lower note up to the pitch of the higher.

**VIBRATO:** The string is vibrated by rapidly bending and releasing the note with the left hand or tremolo bar.

**WIDE OR EXAGGERATED VIBRATO:** The pitch is varied to a greater degree by vibrating with the left hand or tremolo bar.

**SLIDE:** Strike the first note and then slide the same left-hand finger up or down to the second note. The second note is not struck.

**SLIDE:** Same as above, except the second note is struck.

**SLIDE:** Slide up to the note indicated from a few frets below.

**SLIDE:** Strike the note and slide up or down an indefinite number of frets, releasing finger pressure at the end of the slide.

**HAMMER-ON:** Strike the first (lower) note, then sound the higher note with another finger by fretting it without picking.

**HAMMER-ON:** Without picking, sound the note indicated by sharply fretting the note with a left-hand finger.

**PULL-OFF:** Place both fingers on the notes to be sounded. Strike the first note and without picking, pull the finger off to sound the second (lower) note.

**TRILL:** Very rapidly alternate between the note indicated and the small note shown is parentheses by hammering on and pulling off.

**TAPPING:** Hammer ("tap") the fret indicated with the right-hand index or middle finger and pull off to the note fretted by the left hand.

**PICK SLIDE:** The edge of the pick is rubbed down the length of the string producing a scratchy sound.

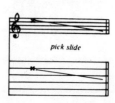

**TREMOLO PICKING:** The note is picked as rapidly and continuously as possible.

**RAKE:** Drag the pick across the strings indicated from low to high with a single downward motion.

**ARPEGGIO:** Play the notes of the chord indicated by quickly rolling them from bottom to top. '

**NATURAL HARMONIC:** Strike the note while the left hand lightly touches the string over the fret indicated.

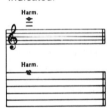

**ARTIFICIAL HARMONIC:** The note is fretted normally and a harmonic is produced by adding the edge of the thumb or the tip of the index finger of the right hand to the normal pick attack. High volume or distortion will allow for a greater variety of harmonics.

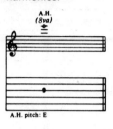

**TREMOLO BAR:** The pitch of the note or chord is dropped a specified number of steps then returned to the original pitch.

**PALM MUTING:** The note is partially muted by the right hand lightly touching the string(s) just before the bridge.

**MUFFLED STRINGS:** A percussive sound is produced by laying the left hand across the strings without depressing them and striking them with the right hand.

**RHYTHM SLASHES:** Strum chords in rhythm indicated. Use chord voicings found in the fingering diagrams at the top of the first page of the transcription.

**RHYTHM SLASHES (SINGLE NOTES):** Single notes can be indicated in rhythm slashes. The circled number above the note name indicates which string to play. When successive notes are played on the same string, only the fret numbers are given.

**NOTE:** Tablature numbers in parentheses mean:

1.  The note is being sustained over a barline (note in standard notation is tied), or

2.  The note is sustained, but a new articulation (such as a hammer-on, pull-off, slide or vibrato) begins, or

3.  The note is a barely audible "ghost" note (note in standard notation is also in parentheses).

## Definitions of Musical Symbols

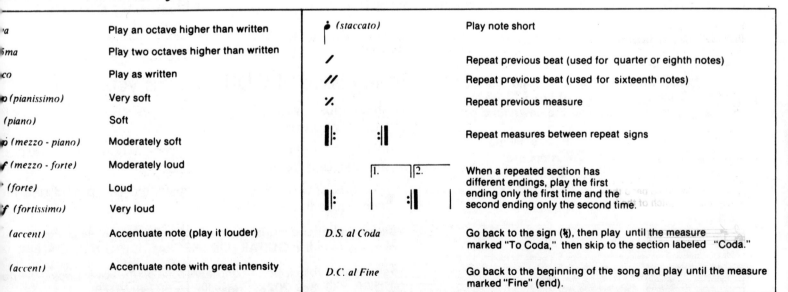

| | | | |
|---|---|---|---|
| *va* | Play an octave higher than written | **●̇** *(staccato)* | Play note short |
| *ma* | Play two octaves higher than written | **/** | Repeat previous beat (used for quarter or eighth notes) |
| *co* | Play as written | **//** | Repeat previous beat (used for sixteenth notes) |
| *(pianissimo)* | Very soft | **%** | Repeat previous measure |
| *(piano)* | Soft | ‖: :‖ | Repeat measures between repeat signs |
| *(mezzo - piano)* | Moderately soft | | |
| *(mezzo - forte)* | Moderately loud | ⌐1.⌐ ⌐2.⌐ | When a repeated section has different endings, play the first |
| *(forte)* | Loud | ‖: \| :‖ \| | ending only the first time and the second ending only the second time. |
| *(fortissimo)* | Very loud | | |
| *(accent)* | Accentuate note (play it louder) | *D.S. al Coda* | Go back to the sign (%), then play until the measure marked "To Coda," then skip to the section labeled "Coda." |
| *(accent)* | Accentuate note with great intensity | *D.C. al Fine* | Go back to the beginning of the song and play until the measure marked "Fine" (end). |

# SPEND A YEAR WITH

**THE BEST SELLING GUITAR MAGAZINE IN AMERICA!**

JULY, 1990

*guitar*

FOR THE ___ MUSICIAN

48429 • $3.50 IN USA • $4.50 IN CAN. • £2.30 IN U.K.

**STEVE VAI**
TRANSCRIPTION TO
CALL IT SLEEP
BASS LINE INCLUDED

**STEELY DAN**
TRANSCRIPTION TO
MY OLD SCHOOL

**KISS GUITARISTS**
POSTER FEATURE
TRANSCRIPTION TO
FOREVER
BASS LINE INCLUDED

**JOHNNY MARR**
TRANSCRIPTION TO
BIGMOUTH STRIKES AGAIN
BASS LINE INCLUDED

**THE NEW METAL**
TRANSCRIPTION TO
SAVATAGE'S GUTTER BALLET
BASS LINE INCLUDED

**YNGWIE MALMSTEEN:
GUITAR TECHNIQUES**
EXCERPTS FROM
ICARUS DREAM SUITE

Eddie Van Halen
Steve Vai
Randy Rhoads
Yngwie Malmsteen
Jimi Hendrix
Vinnie Moore
Stevie Ray Vaughan
Guns N' Roses
Jeff Watson
Carlos Santana
Neal Schon
Eric Clapton
Jimmy Page
Jake E. Lee
Brad Gillis
George Lynch
Metallica
Keith Richards
Jeff Beck
Michael Schenker ...

# AND SAVE $14.00 off the newsstand price!

Just $27.95 buys you a year's subscription to GUITAR and the chance to spend 12 months studying the techniques and the artistry of the world's best guitar performers.

*Get started . . . mail the coupon below!*

☐ **YES! Enter my one-year subscription to** *Guitar for the Practicing Musician* **at just $27.95 for 12 issues —a** *saving of 33%* **off the newsstand price.**

798CL1

☐ Payment enclosed.    ☐ Please bill me.
☐ Charge my   ☐ Visa   ☐ MasterCard
Acct # _____ Exp. Date _____
Signature _____
Name _____
Address _____
City _____ State _____ Zip _____

Outside USA add $15 for postage. Please allow 6-8 weeks for subscription to begin. Send check or money order (no cash) payable to Guitar Magazine. U.S. funds only.
Mail coupon to:    Guitar for the Practicing Musician
                   P.O. Box 2078, Knoxville, IA 50198-7078

**Every issue of GUITAR gives you:**

• sheet music you can't get anywhere else—with accurate transcriptions of the original artists.

• in-depth interviews with guitar greats who candidly discuss the nuts and bolts of what they do.

• columns and articles on the music, the equipment and the techniques that are making waves.

Become a better guitarist and performer. Study with the professionals every month in GUITAR FOR THE PRACTICING MUSICIAN.

To start your subscription — *and save 33% off the cover price* — write GUITAR, P.O. Box 2078, Knoxville, IA 50198-7078